1 The variety of living things

Introduction

There are millions of different living things on the Earth. They can be divided into two main groups, **plants** and **animals**. They live in every kind of place you can think of.

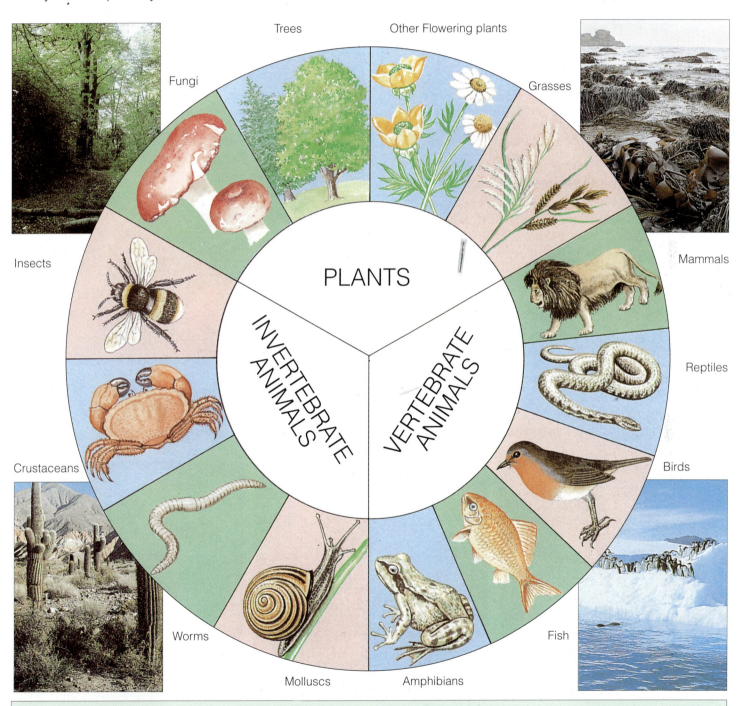

Q1 What are the two main groups of animals called?	**Q3** Which group do you think each of these living things fit into
Q2 Which animal group do you think we belong to?	**a** mushrooms? **b** slugs? **c** butterflies?

1 The variety of living things

Variety

All living things have several things in common.

They feed

They move

They are aware of their surroundings

As well as this they all **grow** and **breathe**. They all have to get rid of **body wastes**. They must all **reproduce**. Animals and plants that are not able to reproduce will die out (become **extinct**). Many living things such as dinosaurs have become extinct.

Reproduction of living things

Plants and animals reproduce in different ways.

Some plants reproduce by making seeds

Some animals lay eggs

Some animals have babies that grow inside them

Q1 What do all living things have in common?

Q2 Choose one plant or animal that you know well. Write a few sentences about how it lives.

Q3 Think of three animals that reproduce very differently. Write a few sentences about how each reproduces.

2 Plant reproduction

Flower structure

This cutout will help you to find the different parts of a flower.

Apparatus
- ☐ flower cutout
- ☐ scissors
- ☐ glue
- ☐ colouring pens
- ☐ paper

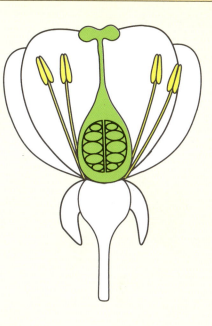

A Colour the male parts of the flower yellow, and the female parts green. Cut out all the parts. ▲

B Stick all the parts of the flower onto the paper like this. ▲

C Learn the names of the different parts so you will be able to find them in real flowers. ▶

Parts of a flower
The **stamens** are the male parts of the flower. The **pollen** is made in the stamens. The **carpel** is the female part of the flower. The **ovules** are made in the carpel. The pollen and ovules are the plant's reproductive cells. Most plants have male and female reproductive parts in one flower.

Q1 What is the male reproductive cell of a plant called?

Q2 Where would you find the female reproductive cell of a plant?

2 Plant reproduction

Looking at flowers

In this experiment you can look for the parts of a flower that you saw on the cutout.

Apparatus
- ☐ flowers ☐ paper
- ☐ tweezers
- ☐ magnifying lens
- ☐ sticky tape

Q1 Copy this table.

Flower	Sepals		Petals		Stamens		Carpels	
	number	colour	number	colour	number	colour	number	colour

A Examine your flower with a magnifying lens. ▲

B Remove the petals and sepals from your flower. Stick them on your paper. ▲

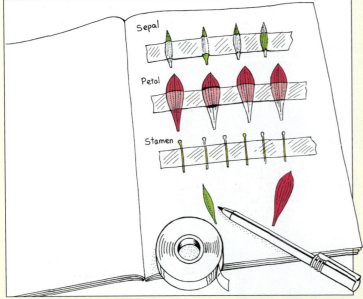

C Remove the stamens from your flower. Stick them on your paper. ▲

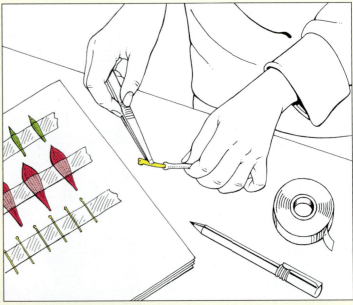

D Remove the carpel from your flower. Stick it on your paper. ▲

E Repeat **A–D** with the other flowers. Stick each flower on a *different* part of the paper. Fill in the table to show the colour and number of the different parts of your flowers.

Q2 Your flower needs to attract insects. Suggest two ways it does this.

2 Plant reproduction

Looking at plant reproductive cells

In this experiment you can examine the pollen and ovule of a flower.

Apparatus
- microscope ☐ tweezers
- microscope slide ☐ cover slip
- mounted needle ☐ flower
- scalpel ☐ pollen grain slide

Safety Warning
Take care when using the scalpel.

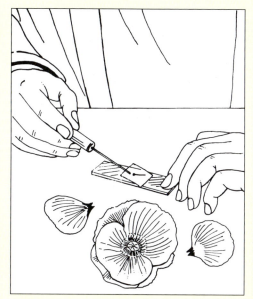

A Put one stamen on a slide with a drop of water. Put a cover slip over the stamen and press it down gently. ▲

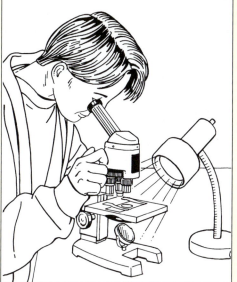

B Examine the stamen with the low power lens of your microscope. Look for the pollen grains. ▲

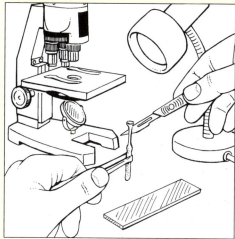

C Remove the carpel from the flower. Cut it down the middle. Put it cut side up on the slide. Look at the ovules with and without the microscope. ▲

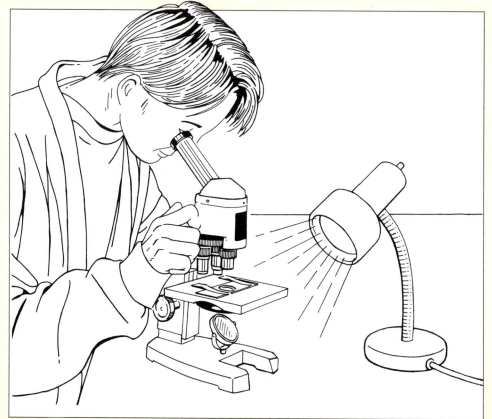

D Use your microscope to examine the slide of different pollen grains. ▲

Q1 Draw a diagram of the carpel in **C**.

Q2 How many ovules did you see in your plant's carpel?

Q3 How many pollen grains did you see in the stamen?

Q4 Some pollen grains are carried by the wind and some by insects. Using the slide of different pollen grains draw a diagram of a pollen grain that you think is
a carried by insects **b** carried by the wind.
Give one reason for your choice in **Q4 a** and **b**.

2 Plant reproduction

Reproductive cells (gametes)

To make a seed, the male **gamete** must join with the female gamete. Gamete is the name for the reproductive cells.

▲ With some plants the wind carries pollen from one plant to another.

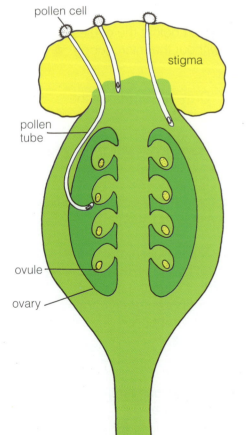

▲ With other plants, pollen is carried by insects from one flower to another.

◀ When pollen reaches the new flower some lands on the **stigma**. This is called **pollination**. The pollen grain grows a tube down to the ovary and the male and female gametes join. This is **fertilisation**. A seed is made. When the seed grows it will be a new plant.

Q1 What is meant by pollination?

Q2 What is meant by fertilisation?

Q3 Look at the photographs at the top of this page showing wind and insect pollinated flowers. Describe two differences between the two types of flowers.

2 Plant reproduction

Asexual reproduction

You have seen how the male and female cells join to make a seed. We call this **sexual reproduction**. Some plants can reproduce without special reproductive cells, this is **asexual reproduction**.

Strawberries, spider plants, potatoes and daffodils reproduce in this way. The new plant grows from an ordinary part of the parent, like a new strawberry plant on the end of a long stem. Gardeners use this knowledge to grow new plants. They cut off a leaf or part of a stem and plant it in soil. Geraniums can be grown from stem cuttings like this.

▲ The gardener cuts a length of stem about 6–10 cm long. She removes two or three lower leaves. Then she plants it firmly in potting compost.

Growing plants from cuttings

Find out if the length of cutting makes any difference to the success of the new plant.

Remember to make your experiment a fair test:
- How many different stem lengths are you going to try?
- Will you cut the stem above or below a leaf joint?
- How will you make sure the cuttings have the same growing conditions?
- How often will you look at your experiments?
- How will you decide which plant is best?

Apparatus

- scalpel
- scissors
- plant pot
- potting compost
- labels

Safety Warning
Take care when using the scalpel.

A In your group discuss what you are going to do. Write out your plan. Ask your teacher to check your experiment for safety before you start. ◀

Q1 Which length of stem grew into the best plant?

Q2 How did you decide which plant was best?

Q3 If you did this experiment again how could you improve your tests?

3 Human reproduction

Reproductive organs   Peter and Shirley have decided they want to have a baby.

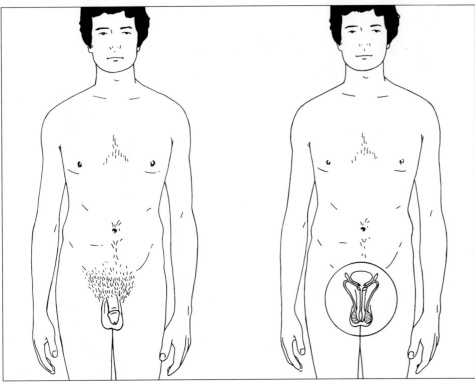

◀ This is what Peter's reproductive organs are like.
The male reproductive organs make **sperm** and place them into the female.
The sperm are made in coiled tubes in the testes. During **intercourse** the sperm pass through the sperm tube in the **penis**.

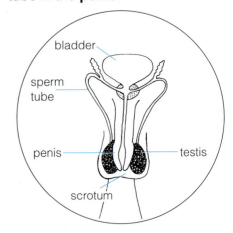

◀ Shirley's reproductive organs are like this.
The female reproductive organs make **ova**. They provide a safe place for the baby to develop. The ova are made in the **ovaries**. When one ovum is fertilised by a sperm a baby develops in the **uterus**.

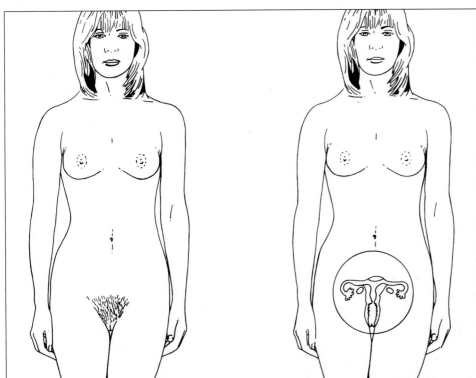

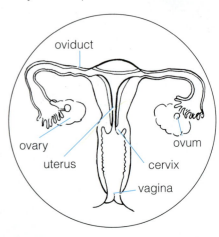

Q1 Where are Peter's sperm cells made?

Q2 Where are Shirley's ova made?

Q3 Where does the baby grow and develop?

3 Human reproduction

Human reproductive cells

In chapter 2 you looked at the reproductive cells (gametes) of plants. In this section you will look at human gametes.

Apparatus
- [ ] ovum and sperm drawing
- [ ] ruler

Q1 Copy this chart.

	Size of drawing	Magnification	Actual size = $\frac{\text{drawing size}}{\text{magnification}}$
Ovum			
Sperm cell			

A Measure the size of the **ovum** and sperm cells. ▲

B Write your results in your chart. Use a calculator to work out the *actual* size. ▲

Intercourse

▶ When they are sexually excited Peter's penis is stiff and erect and Shirley's vagina relaxes and is wet. The movement of Peter's penis inside Shirley's vagina causes their **orgasms**. A white liquid is released from Peter's penis. The liquid contains millions of sperm cells. This is called sexual intercourse (making love). When Peter's sperm joins Shirley's ovum a baby can develop.

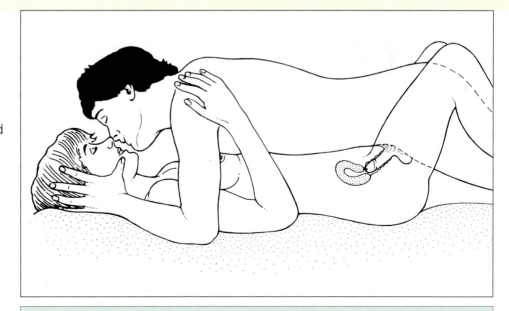

Q2 In real life which cell is the bigger?

Q3 Why do you think this cell needs to be bigger?

Q4 What does the sperm cell shape remind you of?

Q5 Why do you think the sperm cell is this shape?

3 Human reproduction

Conception

After intercourse sperm cells swim from the top of the vagina to the oviduct. Many sperm do not get there. One sperm will join with the ovum. This is fertilisation. The fertilised cell is called a **zygote**. The zygote moves down the oviduct to the uterus where it is implanted in (sticks to) the uterus wall.

Development of the baby

▼ These photographs show the development of their baby during **pregnancy**. The size and mass (weight) of the baby at each stage are shown.

| 5 weeks | 8 weeks | 16 weeks | 32 weeks |

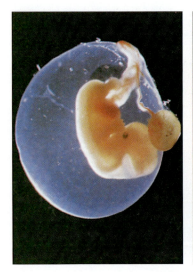 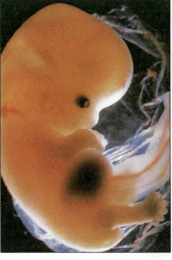 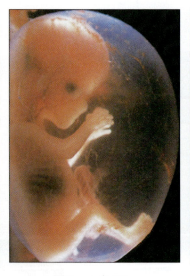 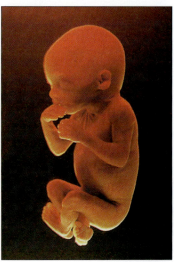

| 12 mm / 0.5 g | 30 mm / 3.5 g | 200 mm / 100 g | 450 mm / 1300 g |

After 40 weeks the baby is born. It weighs about three kilograms and is about 500 mm long.

Q1 In which part of the female
a is the sperm released?
b is the ovum fertilised?
c does the baby develop?

Q2 How many sperm are needed to fertilise an ovum?

Q3 Why do you think millions of sperm are released at a time?

Q4 Write about the path a sperm cell must take to reach the ovum. (**Hint:** see page 8.)

Q5 Make a table to show the changes in the size and mass of the baby as it develops.

Q6 Draw a graph to show the change in mass of the baby during pregnancy.

Q7 Write about the way a baby develops during pregnancy. (Use the photographs above to help you.)

Pregnancy and birth

As the zygote moves down the oviduct it grows and divides, first into two and then four, eight and sixteen cells. At this stage the cells are **unspecialised**. By the time they reach the uterus the cells that are produced have special jobs. The cells have become **specialised**. As the growth continues cells are produced that will develop into muscle cells, nerve cells, blood cells and all the different kinds of cell needed to make a new individual.

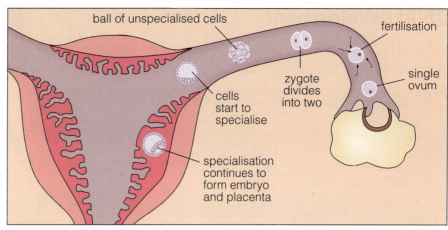

While the **fetus** (baby) is developing in the uterus it needs food and **oxygen** to grow. These pass from Shirley's blood to the blood of the fetus by passing across the placenta and down the **umbilical cord**. During the pregnancy the fetus is protected by the uterus and the bag of fluid that it grows in.

◀ After about 40 weeks the baby is ready to be born. It usually turns head down, Shirley's vagina and cervix get wider and the muscles in the uterus and **abdomen** push the baby out.

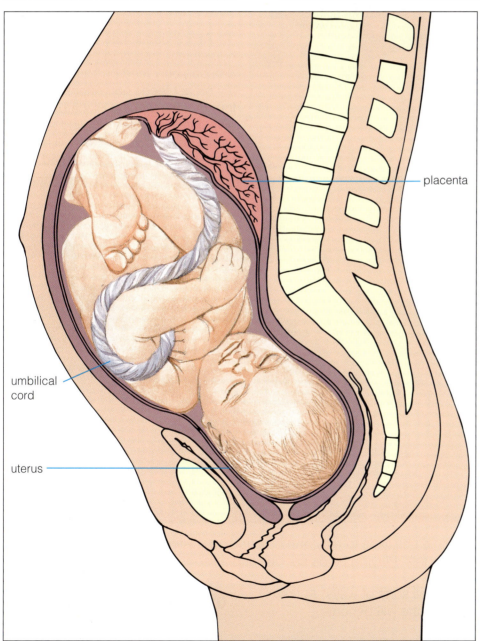

Q1 What is meant by:
a cell growth **b** cell division
c cell specialisation?

Q2 How does the developing fetus get food and oxygen during pregnancy?

Q3 How is the baby protected during pregnancy?

Extension exercise 1 can be used now.

3 Human reproduction

Child development

Viv and Richard planned their baby and they had lots of things ready for her. They called their baby Jamie Lee.

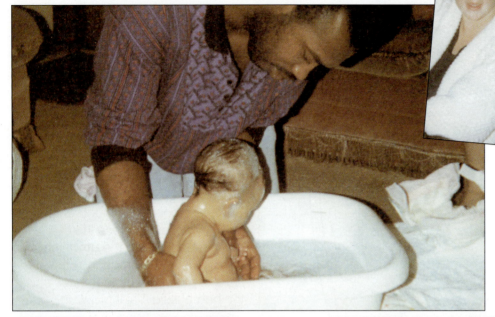

◀ At first Jamie Lee can't sit up by herself, she needs to be supported. She can only feed on liquids and Viv breast feeds her. After about four months Viv and Richard start to give Jamie Lee some solid food. As Jamie Lee grows up they will make sure she has a good **balanced diet**.

▲ As Jamie Lee grows her bones get harder. She starts to roll about and crawl. Eventually she will learn to balance and walk.

▲ Jamie Lee likes to play and be cuddled. Listening helps Jamie Lee learn to talk. Playing helps her develop all sorts of skills.

Richard and Viv help Jamie Lee to develop in all sorts of ways. At first she relies on them totally but as she gets older she will become **independent**.

Q1 Write about all the ways Richard and Viv should care for Jamie Lee to help her grow up happy and healthy.

3 Human reproduction

Puberty

When Jamie Lee is about ten years old changes start to take place in her body. These changes happen in all boys and girls. This part of your life is called **puberty** or **adolescence**. It is the time when your body changes from a child's to an adult's. The changes start between 8 and 18 years old. The changes are caused by chemicals made in the body. These chemicals are called **hormones**. The male hormone is called **testosterone**. The female hormone is called **oestrogen**.

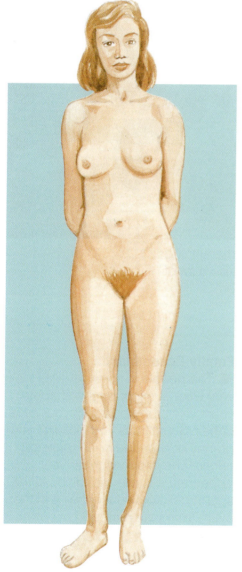

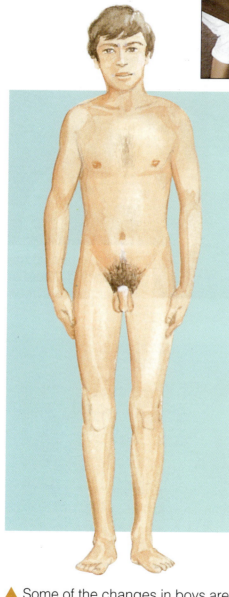

▲ The hormones cause **emotional** as well as physical changes. Boys and girls get more interested in each other. They start to develop and explore new relationships and become aware of sexual feelings. It is important that you take responsibility for your own sexual behaviour.

Casual sexual behaviour could lead to pregnancy, cervical cancer, Aids and sexual diseases.

▲ Some of the changes in girls are:
- increase in height
- breasts grow
- hips get wider
- underarm and pubic hair grow
- periods start
- ova are released from the ovaries.

▲ Some of the changes in boys are:
- increase in height
- shoulders get wider
- voice deepens
- penis and testes get bigger
- sperm cells are made
- underarm, pubic and facial hair grow.

What do you think is responsible sexual behaviour for a person of your age?

Discuss this with your group.

Q1 Write a list of the physical changes that take place during puberty in
a a boy **b** a girl.

Q2 Describe some of the emotional changes that might affect boys and girls during puberty.

4 Variation and inheritance

Introduction

In any group of living things there are a lot of differences between the individuals.

▲ These people have many things in common. There are also a lot of differences between them.

▲ These animals are all cats. There is a lot of **variety** in size, colour and fur.

Family Resemblance

◀ The people in some families look very alike. It might be the shape of your nose or the colour of your eyes or hair. Sometimes you look like your granny or grandad or an uncle or auntie. The information for your appearance is passed to you in the sperm cell from your father and the ovum from your mother.

Q1 List as many differences as you can see between the people in the photograph.

Q2 How are characteristics such as eye colour passed to you?

4 Variation and inheritance

Looking at the differences between people

In this activity you are going to examine several features that vary from one person to another.

Apparatus
- ☐ results table ☐ ruler

A Work with a partner. Fill in all your results as you go. Complete the first line of your table for a male or female. ▲

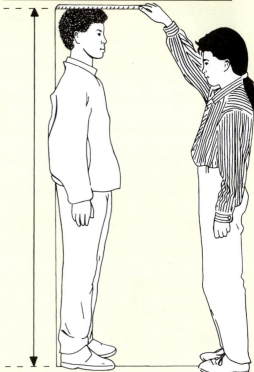

B Measure your partner's height. ▲

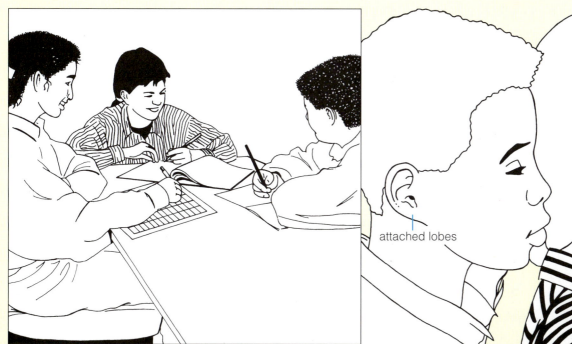

C Look at their skin colour, hair colour and eye colour. ▲

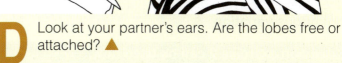

D Look at your partner's ears. Are the lobes free or attached? ▲

4 Variation and inheritance

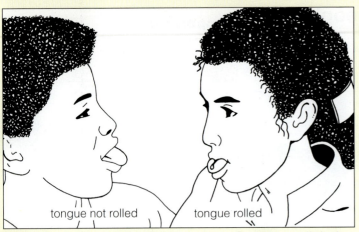

E Look at your partner's tongue. Can they roll their tongue or not? ▲

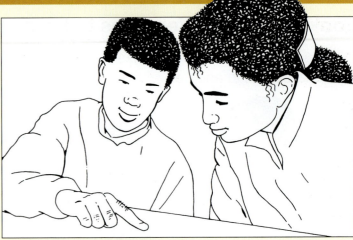

F Look at the middle joint of one of your fingers. Has it got hair on it? ▲

G Try to think of some other characteristics to add to your survey. Collect everybody's results. Complete your results table. ▲

Some of the features you have looked at are either one thing or another (for example, sex and eye colour). This is called **discontinuous variation**. ▲

Other differences vary gradually (for example, height and weight). This is **continuous variation**. ▲

Q1 List the things you looked at that showed discontinuous variation.

Q2 List the things you looked at that showed continuous variation.

Q3 Draw a bar graph to show the variation in:
a height
b eye colour.

Q4 How do you think any of these characteristics could be changed during the person's life?

Extension exercise 2 can be used now.

4 Variation and inheritance

Fruit flies

The variation you have seen between members of your class also occurs in other plant and animal groups.

Q1 Copy this results table.

	Eyes	Wings	Body
Fly 1			
Fly 2			

Apparatus

- tube of fruit flies
- brush ☐ Petri dish
- binocular microscope *or* magnifying lens

 Handle the fruit flies carefully.

A Put all the flies into the Petri dish. Use the brush to move the flies about. ▲

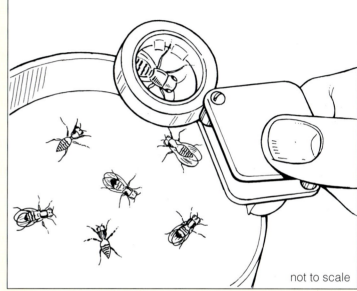

B Look at the first fly. Look at the eyes, the wings and the body. Complete your results table. ▲

C Repeat **B** for the other flies.

Variation

 Variations are passed from parents to **offspring**. Dogs always have puppies not kittens. The puppies will get characteristics from the mother and father. Some puppies will look like the father, some will look like the mother and some will be a mixture.

Q2 How many variations in body colour did you find?

Q3 What were the variations in the fruit fly's wings?

Q4 Which of the characteristics shown by the puppies have been passed from the mother?

4 Variation and inheritance

Chromosomes

▶ You have seen that the variations between individuals are passed from the mother and father to their offspring. The sperm and ova contain the information that makes the new individual. The information for each variation is carried on **chromosomes**. Chromosomes are thread-like structures inside every cell. The picture shows the chromosomes in a human cell.

▼ Chromosomes carry all the information needed for the development of a new plant or animal. Chromosomes are always in pairs. Different sorts of plants and animals have different numbers of chromosomes. Every hen has 18 pairs of chromosomes in each body cell.

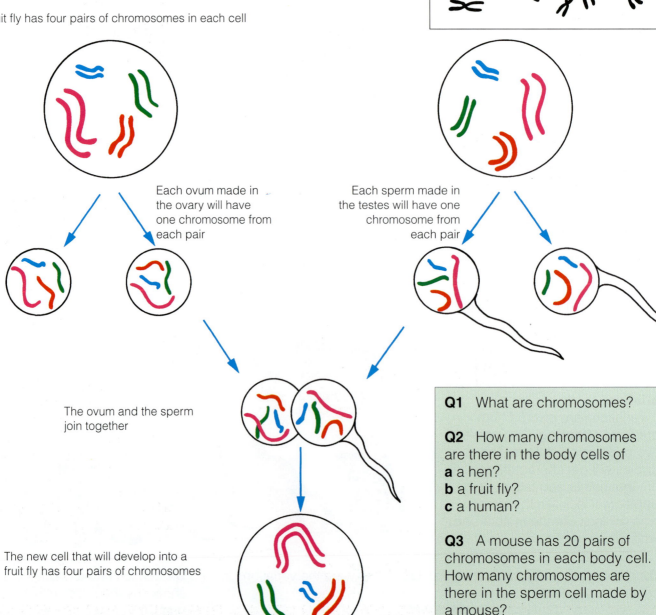

The fruit fly has four pairs of chromosomes in each cell

Each ovum made in the ovary will have one chromosome from each pair

Each sperm made in the testes will have one chromosome from each pair

The ovum and the sperm join together

The new cell that will develop into a fruit fly has four pairs of chromosomes

Q1 What are chromosomes?

Q2 How many chromosomes are there in the body cells of
a a hen?
b a fruit fly?
c a human?

Q3 A mouse has 20 pairs of chromosomes in each body cell. How many chromosomes are there in the sperm cell made by a mouse?

4 Variation and inheritance

Kangaroo chromosomes

In this experiment you can learn about the chromosomes in the cells of a kangaroo.

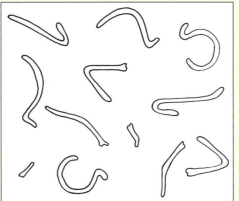

◀ Female kangaroo chromosomes in a skin cell.

Apparatus

☐ 2 kangaroo chromosome cutout sheets ☐ glue
☐ paper ☐ scissors
☐ 6 different coloured pens

A Cut out the chromosomes from one sheet. Arrange them in pairs. Stick them onto a sheet of paper. ▲

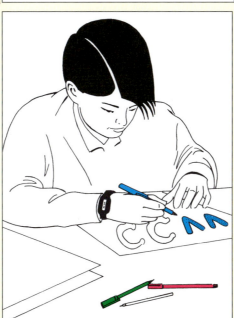

B Colour each pair a different colour from the rest. ▲

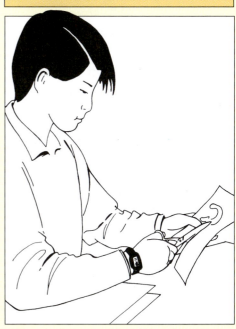

C Cut out the chromosomes from the second sheet. ▲

D On another sheet of paper draw a large diagram of an ovum. Choose the chromosomes that would be in an ovum. Stick them inside the diagram. ◀

Q1 How many chromosomes are in a kangaroo skin cell?

Q2 How many chromosomes are in a kangaroo sperm cell?

Extension exercise 3 can be used now.

4 Variation and inheritance

Genes

Each characteristic, like fruit fly wing shape, is controlled by sections of a pair of chromosomes. The sections of the chromosomes are called genes.

▶ This is a pair of fruit fly chromosomes. You can see where the genes controlling wing shape and body colour are. In between are genes controlling other characteristics. Wing shape is controlled by one pair of genes.

The fruit fly in this diagram has two different genes for wing shape. One gene is for normal wings and the other is for curly wings. Other fruit flies will have two genes for normal wings or two genes for curly wings.

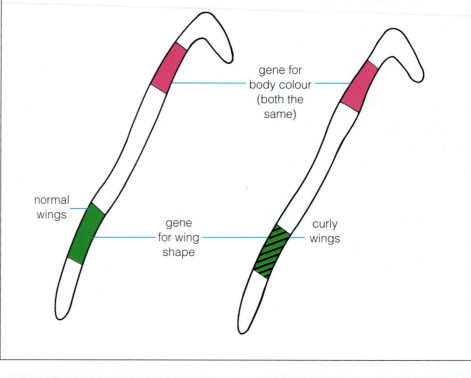

Mutation

Sometimes a gene or group of genes can change. This is called a **mutation**. Missing genes, extra genes or different genes will affect the person, animal or plant. Nearly all mutations are harmful. Many mean death. A few mutations are useful and lead to a change in an animal or plant that is passed to its offspring.

Mistakes in genes can happen naturally but are more common if the animal or plant is exposed to **radiation** or certain chemicals.

▲ This fruit fly has normal wings.

▲ This fruit fly's wings show a mutation: they are very small.

These mutations are more likely to appear if the fruit fly's parents have been exposed to radiation. Fruit flies showing these wing mutations would not survive in the wild. They would not be able to fly.

▲ This fruit fly's wings show a mutation: they are curly.

Q1 What is a gene?

Q2 What is a mutation?

Q3 What is likely to make mutations in animals or plants more common?

4 Variation and inheritance

Height in maize plants

Maize is the plant that produces sweet corn. It is used to make cornflakes. There are two main types of maize plants, tall and dwarf.

You are going to examine three **generations** of maize plants, the parents, the first generation and the second generation.

▶ Pollen from parent plant 1 was transferred to parent plant 2. The seed was collected and grown. These are the first generation plants. The first generation plants pollinated each other and the seeds were grown to give the second generation plants.

Looking at maize plants

Q1 Copy this table.

	Height of plant	Number of leaves	Length of leaves
Parent 1			
Parent 2			
First Generation			

Apparatus

- ☐ parent plants ☐ first generation plants
- ☐ second generation plants
- ☐ ruler

A Examine both parent plants. Measure their height. Count and measure the leaves. Complete your results table. ▼

Q2 Describe the differences between the two parent plants.

4 Variation and inheritance

B Repeat **A** with the plants of the first generation. Complete your results table. ▲

C Examine the second generation. Count the tall and dwarf plants. ▼

Q3 Which parent plant did the first generation plants look like?

Q4 Make a table to show the results of the second generation plant count.

Q5 How many second generation plants looked like parent 1?

Q6 How many second generation plants looked like parent 2?

Q7 How many tall plants were there to every dwarf plant in the second generation?

Q8 Explain why some of the plants in the second generation looked like their grandparents and not their parents.

4 Variation and inheritance

Inheritance of height in maize

We know that offspring inherit half their genes from each parent. Maize plants have a gene for height that comes in two forms: tall (T) and dwarf (t).

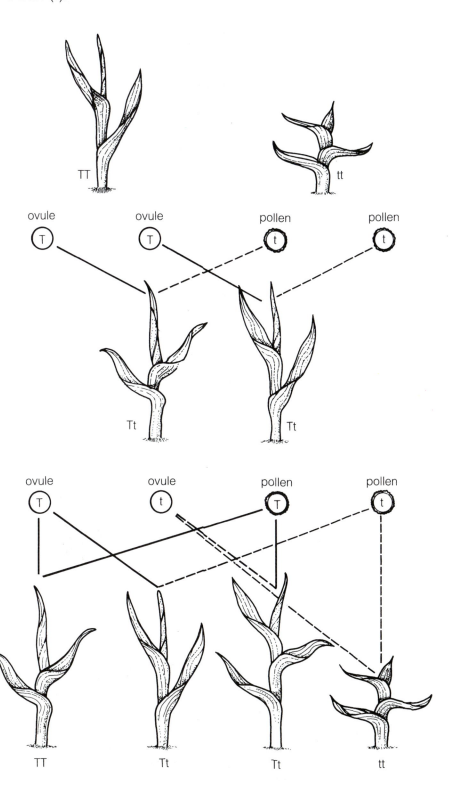

Parent 1 had two genes for tallness. Parent 2 had two genes for dwarfness.

One of each gene went into their ovule and pollen cells.

The pollen and ovule joined together to make the first generation.

These plants had one gene for tallness and one gene for dwarfness. Only the tall gene showed. The characteristic that shows is called the **dominant gene**. The characteristic that does not show is **recessive**.

The first generation genes went into the ovule and the pollen cells.

These joined together randomly. Some second generation plants got two tall genes. Some got one tall gene and one dwarf gene (but looked tall). Some got two dwarf genes.

Q1 Which characteristic for height is dominant in maize plants?

Q2 If a farmer wants to grow a field of dwarf plants, which sort of plants must she collect the seed from?

Q3 If a gardener wants to grow only tall plants, what must she know about the plants that the seeds come from?

4 Variation and inheritance

Other inherited characteristics

All characteristics in animals and plants are controlled by genes. The genes are inherited from the parents in a similar way to height inheritance in maize plants.

▲ Coat colour in mice is inherited. Black fur is dominant to brown fur.

▼ Some characteristics do not have a dominant gene and the young are a mixture of both parents. If a white sweet pea is crossed with a red sweet pea the offspring will be pink. This is co-dominance.

▲ The ability to roll your tongue is also controlled genetically. Tongue rolling is dominant to non-rolling.

▼ Many characteristics are more complicated. They are controlled by a mixture of many genes. Hair and eye colour are two examples of this.

Q1 A male mouse with two black genes mates with a brown female mouse. What colour would the baby mice be?

Q2 David can roll his tongue, but also has a gene for non-rolling. He marries Sharon who cannot roll her tongue. What are the chances of their children being able to roll their tongues?

Q3 Explain what happens if one gene for a characteristic is not dominant to another.

5 Human inheritance

Inheritance of sex

The information that decides whether you are a boy or girl is contained in your chromosomes.

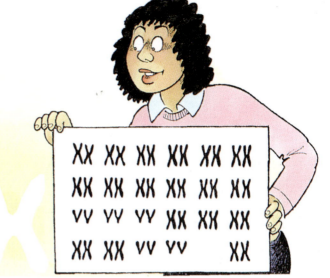

▲ These drawings show the chromosomes of a boy and a girl. They are all the same except the last pair. These are called the X and Y chromosomes. A girl has two X chromosomes. A boy has an X chromosome and a Y chromosome. People still cannot choose the sex of their babies, but we do know how sex is inherited.

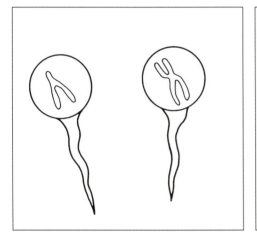

▲ The sperm cells might contain an X chromosome or a Y chromosome.

▲ The ova always contain an X chromosome.

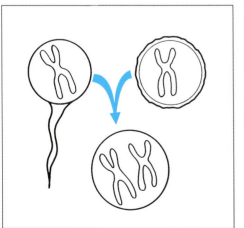

▲ If a sperm containing an X chromosome fertilises the ovum the baby will be a girl.

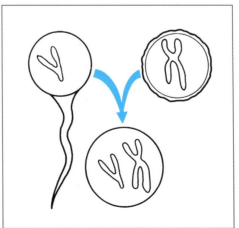

▲ If a sperm containing a Y chromosome fertilises the ovum the baby will be a boy.

Q1 Draw a diagram of the sex chromosomes of a boy and a girl.

Q2 Explain how the sex of a baby is inherited.

5 Human inheritance

Working out the sex of a baby

Apparatus
- ☐ sperm cards ☐ ovum cards
- ☐ 2 bags

In this experiment you will be able to work out the chance of a baby being a girl or a boy.

Q1 Copy this table.

Baby number	Sperm chromosome	Ovum chromosome	Baby's chromosomes	Baby's sex
1				
2				

A Put all the sperm cards into one bag and all the ovum cards in another bag. ▲

B Without looking take a sperm card out of the bag. Write the chromosome type in the sperm column of your table. Put the card back in the bag. Repeat **B** using the ovum bag. ▲

C Repeat **B** and **C** 20 times. Complete the last two columns of your table. ◀

Q2 How many baby boys and how many baby girls did you get in your experiment?

Q3 Mrs. Singh is expecting a baby. What is the chance of her baby being a boy?

Q4 Explain why you would expect equal numbers of baby girls and boys to be born.

Q5 In the future it might be possible to decide the sex of your baby. Do you think this is a good idea? Give reasons for your answer.

5 Human inheritance

Genetic disorders

Genetic disorders happen when something goes wrong with a gene, a group of genes or a chromosome. The change in the gene might have passed through generations of a family or it might be due to change in the reproductive cell.

Down's syndrome, cystic fibrosis, sickle cell anaemia, haemophilia, colour blindness, albinism and Huntington's chorea are all examples of genetic disorders.

Cystic fibrosis is the most common gene-inherited disease in Britain. Children with cystic fibrosis produce sticky mucus in the lungs and the pancreas. This can cause breathing difficulties and digestive problems. There is no cure for cystic fibrosis yet, but a lot of progress has been made in the treatment of the symptoms.

A person who has cystic fibrosis must have two alleles for the disease. If someone has one allele for the disease they are a carrier. They do not have the disease but could pass the allele on to their children.

◀ **Albinism** is caused by a recessive gene that stops the development of skin, hair and eye colour.

▼ **Down's Syndrome** is caused by one extra chromosome in the cells.

Cystic fibrosis can be treated with physiotherapy. ◀

Huntington's chorea is a rare inherited disease. The disease affects the nervous system. It causes uncontrolled movements. The symptoms of Huntington's chorea do not develop until middle age.

Q1 Find out more about information about cystic fibrosis and its treatment.

5 Human inheritance

Colour-blindness

Some genetic diseases are linked to the sex chromosomes. This means that the gene that causes the disease is on the X chromosome but not on the Y chromosome. For a female to get a sex-linked inherited disease, the gene causing the disease would have to be on both chromosomes. Males only have one X chromosome so that if it carries the gene causing the disease, they will have the disease. Males are more likely to have sex-linked inherited diseases.

Haemophilia is a sex-linked inherited disease. People who suffer from haemophilia are not able to produce the chemical that causes the blood to clot. If they are not treated, injuries they get do not stop bleeding normally. The condition cannot be cured but it can be treated with injections of blood-clotting chemicals. Because haemophilia is a sex-linked disease, women can be carriers of the disease but are not affected by it. Queen Victoria, who was born in 1819, was a carrier of haemophilia.

Colour blindness is another sex-linked inherited disorder. People who are colour blind have difficulty seeing the difference between some colours. The most common is red-green blindness.

Charts can be used to test for colour blindness.

Some inherited diseases can be treated but many cannot. People who know they have inherited diseases in their family often go to an expert for genetic counselling. The counsellor will work out the chances of any baby they may have of being affected by a genetic disorder.

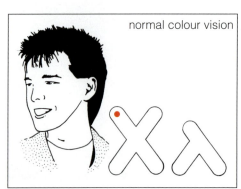

▲ Fred is not colour-blind. He has a normal gene.

▶ Joan is colour-blind. Both her genes are for colour-blindness.

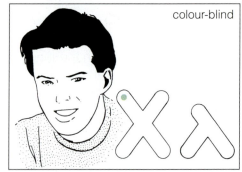

▲ Simon is colour-blind. He has the colour blind gene.

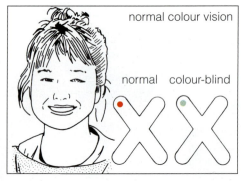

▲ Mary is not colour-blind. She has a normal gene but she carries a gene for colour-blindness.

Q1 Imagine you carried a gene for a disease that could be passed to your children. What would you do? Discuss this in your group.

Q2 What are the symptoms of haemophilia?

6 Genetics in action

Variation and the environment

Some characteristics that are inherited can be changed by the **environment** and others cannot. An animal or plant might contain the genetic message to grow large. If it does not get enough food it will not be able to reach its full size.

▶ Larch trees normally grow to about ten metres. If a larch tree is grown in a small pot it will stay small. This happens naturally if the tree grows on a rock face. Seeds from the small trees will grow to their full size. The inherited message has not been changed.

◀ Sheep are born with long tails. Their tails are cut off (docked) when they are lambs. When the lambs grow up and breed their lambs will have long tails. Cutting off the tails did not change the message for long tails.

Changing to suit the surroundings

▶ In nature animals and plants that are suited to their surroundings do not change much. If the surroundings change, one type of animal or plant becomes more common. Changes in the animal or plant that help it survive will be passed to the offspring.
If the plant or animal is not able to change as fast as its surroundings, it will die. If all the plants and animals of one sort die then they become extinct (there are none left alive). People are changing the surroundings of many plants and animals so much that they are in danger of becoming extinct. Laws are made to protect these plants and animals.

Q1 How is the larch tree changed by its environment?

Q2 Why have some plants and animals become extinct?

Q3 Find out about a plant or animal that is in danger of becoming extinct. What would you do to protect it?

6 Genetics in action

Natural selection

The characteristics of the animal or plant that help it to survive changes in its surroundings will be passed to its offspring. Animals showing this characteristic will become more common. This process is called **natural selection**.

In a rabbit population some rabbits can run faster than others.

Rabbits that run fast will not be caught as easily as slow running rabbits.

The fast running rabbits will live longer and have babies. They pass their fast running characteristic to the next generation.

Fast running becomes more common in rabbits.

Many animal and plant characteristics develop in this way. Pale mice are more easily seen than dark mice. Pale mice are more likely to be caught and eaten by owls. Plants with long roots can reach further for water than plants with short roots. In a dry summer, long rooted plants will live longer.

Q1 Explain how the ability of rabbits to run fast has developed by natural selection.

Q2 Choose one plant or animal that you know about. Write about a characteristic that you think has been changed by natural selection.

Extension exercises 4 and 5 can be used now.

6 Genetics in action

Artificial selection

Ever since people started keeping animals and growing crops they have been keeping the best for breeding. The weaker ones were eaten. All the modern breeds of farm animals have been developed this way. The process is called **artificial selection**.

▲ Today's **cereals** such as wheat have been developed from the grass our **ancestors** ate. Each plant gives much more food.

▲ The wild pig has been changed by breeding programmes into the modern pig we see on farms today.

Farmers and gardeners use genetic knowledge to grow plants and animals that will make the most money. By careful breeding they produce the sort of animal or plant that sells well.

▲ Most families like a lean beef joint. The farmer breeds a quick growing animal instead of the older, slow growing breeds that used to be popular.

▲ By careful breeding programmes, farmers have produced sheep that are more likely to have twin lambs.

Q1 How does a knowledge of genetics help plant and animal breeders?

Q2 Imagine you are keeping sheep for their wool. What characteristics would you look for in the sheep you used for breeding?

6 Genetics in action

Scientific knowledge of plant breeding has been used to grow better crops. Cereals like wheat, barley and rice have been carefully bred. This has helped to reduce food shortage in many areas. Sometimes genetic improvements do not work. High production rice and wheat **varieties** were developed to help overcome **famine** in Asia. Unfortunately the plants were not as **resistant** to disease as the traditional varieties and so they died.

▲ By selecting certain characteristics plant breeders have developed very large and very small tomatoes.

▲ Every year growers breed new varieties of flowers and vegetables that will grow better or look nicer in our gardens.

◀ Racehorse breeders try to breed the fastest and strongest horse possible. Horses that win top races are used for breeding.

Q3 Imagine you are a plant breeder and you want to grow a type of rice that gives high production and is resistant to diseases. You already have some plants that are good producers and some disease resistant plants. Describe what you would do.

Extension exercise 6 can be used now.